Curiosities of Cumbria

We hope you will retain happy memories of "good old Cumbria"

George & Cynthia

Wigton. June 1994.

Cover photograph: Memorial on the wall of Dacre Church
Half title page: The Golden Rule Fish at Ambleside
Back cover: The Black Hog of Stricklandgate

All other photographs are by the author, except for the ones of the Ratty Railway train and the Levens Hall Topiary which are from the Tourist Board, and the Serpent Stone, which is courtesy of the Senhouse Museum.

Curiosities of Cumbria

A County Guide to the Unusual

by

Kat Thurston

S.B. Publications

To Fat and Thin
who have been with me for fifteen years
and who loved the Lake District more than anyone.
Fat is on his last paws, and Thin has already passed
through the great cat-flap in the sky.
Requiscat in Pace

First published in 1994 by S.B. Publications
c/o 19 Grove Road, Seaford, East Sussex BN25 1TP

ISBN 1 85770 058 9

Typeset, printed and bound by Manchester Free Press,
Longford Trading Estate, Thomas Street, Stretford, Manchester M32 0JT

CONTENTS

THE AUTHOR

Kat Thurston was born in 1963. Her first passion was the movies, so she trained as a camera technician in the film industry and worked on many features and commercials, before turning to writing. This second career began with newspaper articles and she is currently working on a screenplay. Kat has travelled extensively, and recently wrote a book about a trip around India on a motorbike. Her latest passion is flying, and she now divides her time between the French Alps and the Lake District, where she can often be seen floating over the fells beneath her paraglider.

Kirkland Tower, Grange

INTRODUCTION

Artists and Poets have always flocked to Cumbria, attracted by the dramatic scenery and constantly changing shadows and moods. Everyone loves the Lake District. Fifteen million visitors come from all over the world to this region each year, but it is now taking its toll. The most popular fells are scarred with eroded paths the width of the M6 motorway. However, most of us live in a noisy and congested urban environment and the need to escape was never greater.

So, what can be done? Some extremists suggest limiting the numbers of visitors, but with the demise of hill farming and other northern industries, the region desperately needs the income from tourism.

The answer is to give people the motivation to explore the far corners of the county, to get them away from the busy heart of the region. It is therefore my intention with this book to draw visitors from the saturated areas and lead them to a discovery of the numerous hidden treasures in Cumbria. The county has an enormous topographical range, from the wild and dramatic western coastline, the large barren hills of the north, the domestic wooded landscape of the south to the bleak expanses of the east.

Searching for curiosities from this book or finding new ones, will take you off the beaten track, give you the opportunity of real encounters with local people, enable you to discover quiet villages, glimpse a simple life-style you thought was abandoned years ago and enjoy the outstanding scenery in a peaceful and positive way.

No one can doubt that there are many people who care and respect the Lake District, and we must support them all we can.

The National Park Authority was set up in 1951 to 'preserve the beauty of the area, and provide for public enjoyment'. The National Trust are spending all their time and energy on way-marking rights of way, planting trees, collecting litter and doing valuable conservation work. The Friends of the Lake District was established in the 1970s to protect the 'natural beauty and character' for all of Cumbria. We are also grateful to English Heritage for all their magnificent efforts in preserving our ancient monuments and historical homes.

Kat Thurston

CUMBRIA

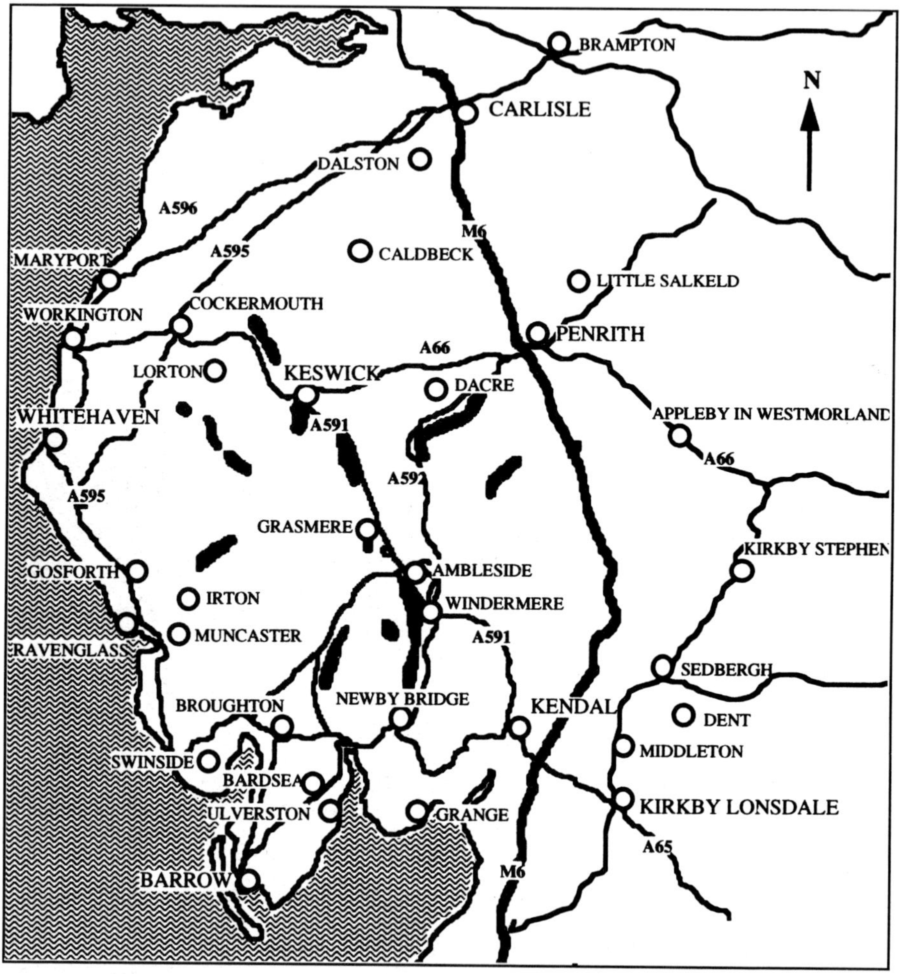

BRAMPTON
N
CARLISLE
DALSTON
A596
M6
CALDBECK
A595
MARYPORT
LITTLE SALKELD
COCKERMOUTH
WORKINGTON
PENRITH
A66
LORTON
KESWICK
DACRE
WHITEHAVEN
A591
APPLEBY IN WESTMORLAND
A66
A592
A595
GRASMERE
KIRKBY STEPHEN
GOSFORTH
AMBLESIDE
IRTON
WINDERMERE
MUNCASTER
A591
RAVENGLASS
SEDBERGH
BROUGHTON
NEWBY BRIDGE
KENDAL
DENT
SWINSIDE
MIDDLETON
BARDSEA
ULVERSTON
GRANGE
KIRKBY LONSDALE
A65
M6
BARROW

MARYPORT

THE SERPENT STONE

Location: The Senhouse Roman Museum, the Sea Brows at the end of the cliff top overlooking Maryport. NY039372

Access: Open July to September, every day, 10am–5pm; November to March, Friday to Sunday only, 10.30am–4pm.

The Roman Fort which stands next to the museum at Maryport was the Headquarters of Hadrians's Coastal Defence system. The Senhouse Roman Museum is full of exciting treasures excavated from here and is said to be the largest and oldest collection of Roman Military Altar Stones and Inscriptions to be found on one site anywhere in the country. It also houses some awesome examples of pagan Celtic sculpture, including Warrior Gods and the striking Serpent Stone.

The serpent Stone was found in 1880 near the fort among the remains of funeral pyres and is thought to be the primative tombstone of a Mithraic cult member. The Stone is over four feet tall and is shaped like a phallus, with a human face on one side and a serpent on the other.

MARYPORT MARITIME MUSEUM

overlooks the recently developed harbour and is on the site where the first building of the town was constructed by Humphrey Senhouse II. The town is named after his wife, Mary. You can discover more about the maritime history of the area including the story of Fletcher Christian and the man whose *White Star Line* built the infamous *Titanic.* There are two restored steamships in Elizabeth Dock, the *Flying Buzzard* and the *Vic 96*.

WORKINGTON

THE CASTLE PIT HEAD

Location:	On the west coast, at the end of the A66 from Cockermouth. NX9928

On the edge of a playing field in this peaceful town, stands a derelict tower and two castellated chimneys, known locally as 'The Castle'. It overlooks a quiet housing estate and it is difficult to imagine the noise and bustle which used to take place here. This was once the entrance of Jane Pit where coal was mined from 1844. Across the road was the entrance to another colliery, Annie Pit, which was closed up because of subsidence and now lies beneath the Territorial Army building.

WORKINGTON HALL is worth a visit whilst you're in the area. This ruin stands outside the town above the River Derwent, and hides a sad story of neglect and decay. It was once one of the finest houses in Cumberland and where Mary Queen of Scotts took refuge in 1568. It was the home of the Curwen family for over six centuries, before they gave the Estate to the local authority when they moved to Belle Isle, on lake Windermere. Thus started its decay into dereliction. In the 1970s the Royal Commission on Historical Monuments stepped in with a small grant to make it into a 'safe ruin'.

WHITEHAVEN

CASTELLATED MINE SHAFTS

Location:	On the west coast, overlooking Whitehaven Harbour. NX967177

There were once 120 deep coal mines in this coastal area. The last deep mine, Haig, (to the south) closed in 1985. It is amazing to think that the workings extended up to 5 miles beneath the sea.

In the 18th century the first Earl of Lonsdale constructed many of his colliery buildings in this coal port town to look like little castles. On the cliff overlooking the harbour stands the fan house. It is now preserved as a memorial to the hundred miners who were killed in an underground explosion.

A few minutes walk back along the sea front, brings you to Wellington Lodge. This is a castellated tower which was the entrance to the Wellington Pit, 'sunk in 1840, closed in 1933'.

There is also a commemorative plaque on the sea wall which reads:

In memory of the men, women and children who
lost their lives in the Whitehaven District Collieries

It seems shocking to us today to realize that women and children went down the mines.

WHITEHAVEN

THE CANDLESTICK CHIMNEY

Location:	In the town centre

This tall chimney dominates the harbour of Whitehaven, which is now full of little fishing boats and has been declared a conservation area. The chimney is a constant reminder of the times when the harbour was full of large ships being loaded up with coal and iron ore going to locations all over the country. In the 18th century, Whitehaven was the third most important port in Britain, larger than Liverpool. Lord Lonsdale owned most of the mines in the area and had this chimney built like a candlestick, just for a bit of fun. Its function was not to carry smoke, but as a ventilation shaft to bring air down into the mine.

THE WHITEHAVEN MUSEUM concentrates on the Maritime, industrial and social history of the first English 'Planned Town' since medieval times. Among its treasures is the Beilby's 'Slavery Goblet', which commemorates the launch of the Whitehaven-built slave ship 'King George'. It is open from 10am–4.30pm, except Sundays and Bank Holidays.

THE DRINKING FOUNTAIN

There are many fine Georgian houses in Whitehaven, and its affluent era is evident everywhere. On the main street is an interesting iron drinking fountain which has been there since 1869. The water would have come out of the lion's mouth, and collected in the shell just off the pavement, which was probably for dogs to drink from. There is also a Coat of Arms, which appears above doorways all over town.

GOSFORTH

THE VIKING CROSS AND THE FISHING STONE

Location: On the A595 going north from Ravenglass/Muncaster, or from Eskdale and the Hardknott Pass.

The sandstone Gosforth Cross stands over 14ft high in Gosforth churchyard. It is decorated in the Danish Jellinge style, and is covered with carving featuring mythological heroes and legends. The Cross was originally one of four erected around 940AD, when the 'myths of the Nordic gods were giving way to the spread of Christianity'. Several fascinating interpretations of the meaning of the carvings are given in a booklet available in the church.

The Fishing Stone

THE FISHING STONE was originally part of a stone frieze in the chancel of the pre-Norman church, and is now one of Gosforth's greatest treasures. The top half of the stone depicts a hart trampling a serpent, representing Good overcoming Evil. On the bottom half, Thor is out fishing with the giant Hymir for the great Midgard serpent (an evil spirit) using the head of an ox as bait; a scene from a well-known Norse story. What can it all mean? All is revealed in the Church booklet.

GOSFORTH

THE HOGBACK TOMBS

It is said that the man who created these stone carvings, was the most accomplished sculptor of the Viking period. There are two stones, one is called the Saint's tomb and the other is the Warrior's tomb. The Saint's tomb is covered with various carvings of animal heads, with the figure of a man astride the jaw of one of them. They depict the killing of the evil Fenris wolf by Vidar, in the last great battle of the Norse sagas between the gods of Good and Evil (Gotterdammerung). The Warrior's tomb shows two processions of warriors with spears facing each other, representing a truce. On one side there is a 'complex ribbon animal with a drilled eye and head'.

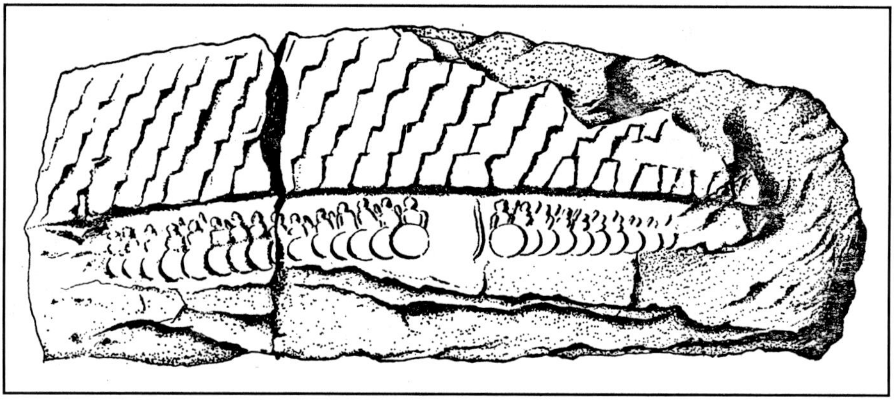

The Warrior's Tomb, Gosforth Church

RAVENGLASS

THE RAVENGLASS AND ESKDALE RAILWAY

Location: On the A595 coast road between Broughton-in-Furness and Whitehaven. SD0996

Access: Trains running daily from April to October, with a reduced service during winter weekends.

The Ravenglass and Eskdale Railway or the 'Ratty', is the oldest narrow gauge steam railway in Britain. It has been taking visitors from the old Roman port of Ravenglass on the coast up the seven mile track to Eskdale for over 100 years.

There is a railway museum at Ravenglass, which brings to life the remarkable history of the railway and its part in valley life. The old Furness railway station here has been converted into a pub, not surprisingly called the Ratty Arms.

At the end of the line, the other station house at Eskdale is now a traveller's café and is the perfect starting point to explore this beautiful area on foot. Wainwright's 'Walks from Ratty' can be bought from the station shop.

MUNCASTER

THE FOLLY AND THE LUCK OF MUNCASTER LEGEND

Location:	On the A595 South East of Ravenglass on the West coast, visible as you approach Muncaster Castle. SD1196

The first Lord Muncaster erected this three-storey stone tower around 1800 to commemorate an important date in the history of his castle. A local shepherd met King Henry VI at this spot fleeing from the Battle of Towton in 1461 and led him to a safe haven in the nearby castle.The famous glass bowl 'The luck of Muncaster' was given by 'Holy King Harry' to the Pennington family, who still have it in their possession. The legend goes that as long as the bowl remains in one piece, the Penningtons will live and thrive at Muncaster Castle. The family still live there today.

The octagonal tower has a pyramidal roof and lancet windows, and stands overlooking the Esk valley at the edge of an ancient wood, a view that John Ruskin once described as 'Heaven's Gate'.

MUNCASTER

THE CASTLE STABLES

Location: On the A595 South East of Ravenglass on the West coast.

Access: Castle, gardens and Owl centre open from March to November, afternoons. Closed Mondays.

The red sandstone stables at Muncaster Castle are very special indeed, not least because there is not a horse in sight. They are screened by a fancy Gothic wall, complete with a tudor arch, quatrefoil windows, castellations and turrets. They were built around 1781. Nowadays it houses a tea room, an aviary and a souvenir shop selling anything decorated with or in the shape of an owl.

THE OWL CENTRE is a breeding and conservation unit with one of the largest owl collections in the world.

MUNCASTER CASTLE itself is worth a visit; it has been the home of the Pennington family since the 13th century, when the original Pele tower was built on Roman foundations. There is also a haunted bedroom, the famous drinking bowl of Henry VI, and a portrait of Thomas Skelton, the 'last fool of Muncaster', who gave us the word 'tomfoolery'.

IRTON

THE 1000-YEAR-OLD CROSS

Location:	Signposted off the A595 from Ravenglass going north.

This Saxon stone cross is in the middle of the graveyard of Irton Church, a beautiful and remote setting. You would probably never come here unless you were looking for this cross and you'd be very glad you did.

The Irton Cross is over 1000 years old, is made of sandstone and is beautifully decorated with Runic inscriptions and swirly sculptured patterns.

Also worth a visit whilst you're in the area is St Olaf's Church at Wasdale Head, said to be the smallest church in England. Carry on from Irton and turn right at Santon Bridge for about eight miles. No-one knows exactly how old the church is, but the valley was inhabited from the 13th century, although the cross at Irton dates three centuries before that.

Among the interesting features of the church are the main roof beams, which are said to have come from a Viking's ship! According to an informative booklet available in the church, the original inhabitants of Wasdale were of Viking descent; the folklore and dialect were all from Scandinavia. Curiously, they brought with them the Herdwick sheep, which you will see everywhere you go, and not just in the fields. The Churchwarden's staves are unique; there is a ram's head on one and a ewe's head on the other.

HARDKNOTT PASS

THE ROMAN FORT

Location:	Overlooking the Upper Eskdale valley. Take the A593 from Ambleside, turn right to Little Langdale, through the Wrynose Pass. NY219014

The Roman Fort at the top of Hardknott Pass is one of the best examples in Britain. The Romans called it Mediobogdum when about 500 soldiers from the Dalmatians regiment were garrisoned here between 90 and 190AD. The Fort was built by the governor Agricola, during the reign of Hadrian, to link the coast with military stations inland via a route right across the fells. The defence line stretched from Fort Galava at Ambleside to the one at Glannaventa or Ravenglass as we now call it.

Hardknott Fort has been restored by the Department of the Environment. The outside walls are 6ft thick and it is no surprise that there are remnants still standing today. You can also see the remains of the Commander's house, the look-out posts, the granary and the administration block. All are clearly labelled to help the imagination. The bath house is the most complete and stands just outside the entrance. It had a sequence of three rooms, cold, warm and hot and a detached circular hot bath, pictured below.

The site is one of the most bleak and dramatic in the Lake District, standing at over 1,200ft, overlooking the Esk Valley and facing out to sea.

SWINSIDE

THE STONE CIRCLE

Location:	2 miles west of Broughton-in-Furness, near Millom. SD1080

This is a ceremonial monument, whose precise ritual function remains a mystery, which makes it much more interesting than if we knew that cock fighting or the weekly market took place here.You can let your imagination run riot; secret witches meeting place, sun or moon worshipers, sacrificial toadstool burials . . .

This evocative. stone circle is at the end of a long track in a farmer's field surrounded by cows and hills.The stones have a diameter of about 150ft and the fifty-five remaining stones are set in a layer of 'rammed pebbles'.

BROUGHTON-IN-FURNESS

FISH SLABS AND STOCKS

Location:	On the A595. NY2187

In the OED, a 'stock' can mean both 'a table or slab on which a fishmonger cuts his goods' and 'an obsolete instrument of punishment, consisting of two planks of wood set edgewise one over the other. The person to be punished was placed in a sitting position with his ankles confined between the two planks.' How sensible, therefore, that both types should be found side by side in village squares.

Nowadays, the main square in Broughton-in-Furness is a quiet and respectable place, but years ago it must have been full of hustle and bustle. The weekly market took place here where local fisherman would lay out their catch on the fish tables, which are still standing beneath a huge chestnut tree.

Right next to them are the wooden stocks, where the village rascals would be knocked down a peg or two in front of all their friends, and where the constant smell of rotting fish must have been torture to their nostrils!

ULVERSTON

COW TRAFFIC LIGHTS

You've heard of zebra crossings, well, this is a cow crossing. The A590 to Barrow has become such a busy road, with a continuous line of lorries at peak times, that Ermentrude and Daisy get dizzy looking left and right waiting to cross. Thoughtfully the local council stepped in to provide them with their very own traffic lights, just for cows!

ULVERSTON

THE MEMORIAL WHICH LOOKS LIKE A LIGHTHOUSE

Location: At the top of Hoade Lane, off the A591 towards Barrow. SD295791

The Hoade Memorial is a light house that never actually was a lighthouse, perched on a hill overlooking Ulverston, which was once a thriving port, but now has no access to the sea. The 100ft-high monument is a copy of the Eddystone lighthouse, designed by A Trimen, and cost £1,250 to build. It commemorates Sir John Barrow, who died in 1848. On the 15th May 1850, Sir John Barrow's two sons laid the foundation stone for this remarkable folly to the accompaniment of the Ulverston Brass Band during a day of much celebration which was reported in the Illustrated London News.

From quite humble origins, Sir John rose to become Under Secretary to the Admiralty during the Napoleonic Wars. He was also a geographer, who travelled to China and South Africa, and was involved in Arctic exploration. Details of Sir John's career can be found on inscriptions inside the monument, where you can also buy souvenirs and refreshments, when the red flag is flying. So if you see the red flag, you will know that it does not mean a danger warning to distant ships, but just that the kettle is on!

Another curiosity is a recent inscription which has been etched crudely into a slab of stone at the entrance. It reads: 'And when you call I will hear you, for my love for you and Everyman will not shatter.' I will leave this one as a mystery for you to solve.

ULVERSTON

CONISHEAD PRIORY AND THE FOLLY TOWER

Location:	South of Ulverston, on the coast route A5087, to Barrow. SD3076

This impressive Victorian monument of the Gothic revival stands in 70 acres of grounds on the shores of Morecambe Bay. It was built in 1821 by Philip Wyatt for Colonel TR Gale Braddyll. Ironically, it cost so much to build, that the whole estate had to be sold off in order to meet the bill! It took 15 years to complete, during which time Braddyll distracted himself with the construction of various follies in the area.

One of these he built overlooking the house on Hermitage Hill, which has recently been lovingly restored. It is an octagonal, machiolated tower with cross arrow slits and a tiny turret.

The estate is now a Mahayana Buddhist Centre, which runs a full programme of meditation classes and lectures. The monks have been gradually restoring the Priory to its former glory, as it sadly had been left to ruin since the 1970s.

BARDSEA

THE MAUSOLEUM

Location:	On the B5087, south of Ulverston. SD2975

Further down the coast you will find the striking Mausoleum which Colonel Braddyll built during his time at Conishead.

It is triangular, set on a round base, with buttresses and little pyramids on top of the corners. There is a recessed arch on each side, one of which houses a sepulchral urn, and a cupola with a lantern light which can be seen for miles around. The location is splendid; overlooking Morecambe Bay and surrounded by the well kept fairways of the Ulverston Golf Course. You can also see the Hoade Memorial standing prominently in the distance.

ROA ISLAND

SEA MARK

Location:	No longer an island, but at the end of the A5087 outside Barrow. SD204602

Two years ago, this wonderful Victorian Sea mark was due to be demolished, until it was saved by the National Heritage, who stepped in to put a preservation order on it.

The tower was used by ships as a 'leading light' to find their bearings, but it no longer has a function.

BARROW-IN-FURNESS

FURNESS ABBEY RUINS

Location: $1^1/_2$ miles north of Barrow on minor road off A590. SD218717

Access: Open daily, April to September; Tuesday to Sunday during October to March

This was once one of the most powerful and prosperous Abbeys in England, which is difficult to imagine because Barrow is in serious decline nowadays as a centre of ship building and industry. The ruins stand isolated on this barren peninsula in the 'Valley of the Deadly Nightshade'. During its four hundred years, the Abbots of Furness exercised a feudal lordship over huge areas of north-west England, including the central Lake District and parts of Yorkshire. Their wealth grew to indecent proportions considering the Cistercian order originally promoted austerity.

The order was also known for its plain architecture, but one look at the ornate stone canopies over the sedilia and the piscina in the presbytery proves that they did not follow strict rules. The magnificent red sandstone ruins still manage to convey something of the grandeur of life in a wealthy Cistercian monastery. You can still see the impressive Norman arches, the columns of the chapter house and admire the sheer scale and splendour of it all. There are even the cupboards in the cloister were the monks stored their books and the stone seats used by the clergy.

The monastery was founded in 1127, by Count Stephen of Mortain, later King of England. The Abbey was built to withstand attacks from Scottish raiders, who made no distinction between religious and secular targets. The monks did not respond to these threats by turning the other cheek, but raised an army. They also built a watch tower to warn their tenant farmers of the enemy approaching. In 1322 the Abbot paid a ransom to Robert the Bruce to preserve the monastery from arson and plunder.

The monastery burned down after Henry VIII's dissolution of the monasteries, then passed into the hands of Thomas Cromwell, then to various families until the Office of Works took it over in 1923.

HOLKER, CARTMEL

THE LARGEST SLATE SUNDIAL IN THE WORLD

Location: Holker Hall, Cark-in-Cartmel on the B5278, 15 mins from the A590 at Newby Bridge. SD360774

Access: Open from April to October, Sunday to Friday.

The world's largest slate sundial, was designed by the Honourable Mark Lennox Boyd MP, to emulate the earliest known sundial invented over 2300 years ago. The dial is five feet in diameter and is marked into fifteen minute divisions for date with six divisions for the twelve signs of the zodiac. The latitude is also marked on the dial, together with a table of correction for GMT. To use the sundial to calculate the time, 'you must first find the days date and add or subtract the time stated to that shown on the dial itself'. It is much quicker to look at your watch!

The sundial is made of durable grey slate, so will survive well into the future to be a curiosity of tomorrow.The Burlington slate is quarried on the Holker Estate. The sundial is situated in the water meadows of the Deer Park at Holker Hall, (pronounced h*oo*ker!) providing you with the perfect motivation for an interesting exploration of this splendid house and its gardens. Also worth a nostalgic visit is the Lakeland Motor Museum, which has over one hundred historical vehicles and displays of unusual automobilia.

CARTMEL

THE PRIORY CHURCH

Location:	Signposted off the A590. SD3878

The Cartmel Priory was founded by the Earl of Pembroke in 1188 for Augustinian Canons, who built the church in late Norman and Perpendicular Gothic style. The church survived the Dissolution of the Monastries, ordered by Henry VIII in 1537, and became the local Parish church.

Unusual features are the church tower, which is set diagonally in the roof, a 13th-century choir stall and a wonderful 15th-century east window with original stained glass.

However, the most curious feature is the Cromwell door, in the south west corner which has holes said to have been made by Parishioners firing at Cromwell's soldiers in 1643. There are a number of memorials in the graveyard to people who drowned crossing Morecambe Bay, which is testimony to the dangerous tides which come in over the sands faster than a horse can gallop.

LINDALE

THE IRON MAN'S OBELISK

Location: Off the A590 to Barrow, near Grange-over-Sands. SD4180

This cast iron obelisk at Lindale crossroads has a plaque commemorating:

John Wilkinson
Iron Master
who died XIV July MDCCCVIII
Age LXXX years

John Wilkinson was an eccentric engineer and industrialist involved in the iron trade. After his death he requested that he should be buried in an all-iron coffin in his garden at Castle Head. However the body was later dug up and re-buried in consecrated ground somewhere in Lindale church, possibly beneath a wall or the floor. The obelisk was removed from Castle Head gardens in June 1863, going to various locations and was even left lying in a hedge for many years, before coming to its present location. In 1984 it was restored after a nationwide appeal was launched to raise the necessary funds. There is a gold bust portrait of the Iron man himself and a gold inscription:

'A lasting testimony to his unceasing labours . . . his life was spent in action for the benefit of man and . . . to the glory of god.'

GRANGE-OVER-SANDS

THE HOSPICE

Location:	Signposted off the A590, between the M6 and Barrow. SD399793

The Vicar of Cartmel, Thomas Remington, built this small tower in 1846 as a haven for cold and weary travellers. Inside it contains three benches around a little fire place and the words of the vicar displayed on the walls:

This hospice of Hampsfell is an open door, a like to welcome rich and poor;
a roomy seat for young and old, where they may screen from the cold.

Three windows that command a view, to north, to west and southward too
a flight of steps requireth care, the roof will show a prospect rare.

Mountain and vale you thence survey, the winding streams and noble bay
the sun at noon the shadow hides, along the east and western sides.

A lengthened chain holds guard around, to keep the cattle from the ground
kind reader freely take your pleasure, but do no mischief to my treasure.

There are stone steps on one side leading to the roof, from where a special panorama can be enjoyed over Old Man Coniston, Helvelyn and the Langdales on one side and Morecambe Bay on the other. You will find it easily after following a well marked foot path up behind Grange-over-Sands; a wonderful walk through woods and open heath land, passing fine examples of Limestone paving, which takes about a half hour.

GRANGE-OVER-SANDS

KIRKHEAD TOWER

Location:	Just south of Allithwaite on the Kirkland Road, a few miles along the coast from Grange. SD3878

This delightful castellated tower dates from the early nineteenth century. It now seems an incongruous setting for a folly, tucked behind a row of modern bungalows in the middle of a cowfield, but it still has the same spectacular views over the Grange Estuary as when first built.

LEVENS HALL

THE SMOKING ROOM

Location: 5 miles south of Kendal on A6, exit 36 off M6. SD497852

Access: Sunday to Thursday, Easter to September

This is not a cosy place where the ham is hung, but a cold little hut made out of twigs (which has now been whitewashed) in the furthest corner of the Estate, to where the men were banished for their post prandial smoke. I'm sure this idea could catch on . . .

Levens Hall is also known for its famous 17th-century topiary and collection of working model steam engines. The house is Elizabethan and was developed from a 13th-century Pele tower.

Don't worry if you see the Pink Lady or the Blue Lady, who are both quite friendly ghosts, or be alarmed if a black dog comes bounding up to you before disappearing! It is said that in the 17th century Levens was won in a gambling debt with the Ace of Hearts and sold to James and Dorothy Grahme for £24,000. If you look above the doorway of the Steam Collection, you will see hearts adorning the spouts with their initials.

SIZERGH CASTLE

THE PELE TOWER

Location: $3^1/_2$ miles south of Kendal, NW of interchange A590/591. SD499881

Access: Open to the public from April to October, Sunday to Thursdays, afternoons only.

A Pele tower is a fortified dwelling built in the border counties of England and Scotland as a protection against hostile invaders. They are solid square buildings with a vaulted ground floor, which was used to shelter the animals, whilst the owner and his family sheltered in the upper part, behind very thick walls. There was no staircase, so access was via a ladder from the outside.

This impressive Pele tower was built in the 14th century, and now houses a tea room. The Castle has been the home of the Strickland family for over 750 years, but is managed by the National Trust.

Apart from the house, it is worth visiting the beautiful gardens, which include the Trust's largest limestone rock garden.

KENDAL

THE BLACK HOG OF STRICKLANDGATE

Location:	East of M6 (J37) on A684. SD5192

Before the days of neon signs, shop keepers put symbols of their trade on the shop fronts to catch passing trade. We are still familiar (just!) with the barber's stripy candy stick, but a hog? What could that mean? The butchers?

Well, no. Just a bristle factory which made brushes. It now looks rather incongruous, jutting out from the wall above an Estate Agents next door to Macdonalds, on this busy high street. In fact Kendal is not only the home to K Shoes and the eponymous Mint cake, but it also once had a flourishing brush-making industry.

Also in Kendal which is an absolute must, is the ABBOT HALL MUSEUM of Lakeland life and Industry. It claims to give an insight into a fast disappearing world, of the working and social life of this unique area. (Open all day, all week in summer, afternoons only in winter.)

Nearby, is the BREWERY ARTS CENTRE, and another very special place full of many curious things is the ODDFELLOWS GALLERY. Here you can browse through the interesting collection of sculpture, ceramics, English watercolours and contemporary Lakeland artists.

KENDAL

THE SNUFF FACTORY

As you turn off the High Street into Lowther Street, you are engulfed in a strong smell of tobacco. Wander further down the street and peer into the windows of Gawith, Hoggarth and Co and you can see snuff being made. At one time, Kendal had a thriving tobacco industry, but this is the only one remaining. You can't miss the 'Tobacco and Snuff Manufacturers' because there is an interesting painted figure above the entrance which will catch your eye.

KENDAL

WHERE CATHERINE PARR WAS BORN.

Location:	On the A591, or J37 from M6. SD522923

Everywhere you go in Kendal, you will catch glimpses of the Castle ruins, perched on a hill above the town and overlooking the Kent valley.

It was the ancient seat of the Barons of Kendal, but through the failure to produce male heirs, it was passed through marriage to the families of Le Brus, Roos, and Parr. The last queen of Henry VIII, Catherine Parr, was born here in 1510. She was first married to Edward Borough, then Lord Latimer before becoming Queen of England in 1543. After Henry's death, she married an old lover, Lord Thomas Sudely. Four husbands give her a marriage record nearly as impressive as Henry the Eighth!

The Castle has been allowed to deteriorate for over a hundred years into the present ruin. Only a section of two towers and a part of the outer wall still stand today.

Just across the Kent river is the Parish Church, which is unusual because of its size; it has four aisles included within the nave and chancel, like the famous church of St. John Lateran in Rome. It dates from the fifteenth century. The tower is 80ft high and has a peal of ten bells.

WINDERMERE

LAKESIDE CARVINGS

Location:	Cragwood Hotel, White Cross Bay, next to Brockhole on Lake Windermere. NY390006. The country house hotel stands in sixteen acres of landscaped Thomas Mawson gardens and has an excellent restaurant using herbs from the garden and wines from its own cellar.

Around 1800, a local carver took it upon himself to carve the names of his mates and those he held in high esteem, onto slabs of rock on the shores of Lake Windermere. They are now hidden in the undergrowth and buried beneath debris and leaves. By etching their names into history, he was giving an original gift to his friends. People will be able to read them and wonder who they were in hundreds of years to come.

WINDERMERE

STORR'S TEMPLE

Location:	At Storr's Hall, on Lake Windermere. SD394944

This is locally known as the Fishing house. It stands at the end of a jetty jutting into Lake Windermere on the shores of Storr's Hall (now a hotel), and has the most spectacular views from its three arched windows. Joseph Gandy constructed the folly in 1804 for Sir John Legard. It has four inscriptions honouring the four Admirals of the fleet, Duncan, St Vincent, Nelson and Howe.

AMBLESIDE

THE LITTLE HOUSE ON THE BRIDGE

Location:	On the A591, at the head of Lake Windermere. NY3704

This is said to be the smallest house in England, and it is certainly built in one of the strangest places; on top of a tiny bridge in Ambleside. Now owned by the National Trust, it is open to the public for souvenirs and information on the Trust's activities in the Lake District.

There is a story that the little house was built by a Scottish family who were trying to avoid paying ground rent, but the truth is that it was built as a summer house to Ambleside Hall. However, although difficult to believe, a family did once live in this small house in Victorian times.

AMBLESIDE

THE FISH THAT WAS TOO BIG FOR ITS BOX

Location: At the Golden Rule pub in the heart of Ambleside. NY3704

This is a real curiosity if ever there was one; a fish in a display case with the head and tail sticking out of either end. It bears a brass plaque reading: 'Stuffed and mounted by John Hargreaves 1992'. The Golden Rule is one of Ambleside's nicest and friendliest pubs, so you can puzzle this one out over a pint with the landlord, John Lockley.

LOW WRAY

JOHN LONGMIRE'S FOLLY

Location: At Wray Castle, on the western shores of Lake Windermere. NY375009

Access: The Castle is not open to the public as it is now used as a radio communications training college. You can wander around the grounds, a public footpath which is part of a popular walk and runs right past the door.

This is one of many follies and artificial ruins lying in the grounds of Wray Castle, a neo-gothic monstrosity built by the eccentric Liverpudlian surgeon, James Dawson. There is a story that Doctor Dawson built the Castle with his wife's money, and when she came to see the finished item, she went in the front door and right out of the back, and never set foot in the building again. The architect was H.P Horner, who was responsible for the unusual gardener's cottage, which forms part of a wall separating the kitchen garden from the castle. Apparently, John Longmire had nothing to do with the folly which bears his name. He lived in Troutbeck and used to carve inscriptions of mottoes and poetry into stone, some of which were used in the folly and the nearby castle. It is now owned by the National Trust.

John Longmire's Folly

Wray Castle

The Gardener's Cottage

FAR SAWREY

THE STATION HOUSE

Location:	Above Far Sawrey on the West side of Lake Windermere, in a National Trust wood. SD3796

Hidden in the woods above Far Sawrey is the Gothic Station Cottage. It was originally a summer-house, built around 1799 by the Rev. William Braithwaite, who called it 'Belle View'. It still has the most spectacular views across Lake Windermere.

Braithwaite made himself very unpopular with Wordsworth, who objected to the planting of 40,000 trees. He wrote this in a Lakes guidebook:

'The pleasure house is happily situated, and is well in its kind, but without intending any harsh reflections on the contriver . . . it may be said that he, who remembers the spot on which this building stands, and the immediate surrounding ground as they were less than thirty years ago, will sigh for the coming of that day when Art, through every rank of society, shall be taught to have more reverence for Nature.'

The house is now sadly, just a ruin, but it is still possible to see the castellated towers, and the two roofless storeys with half a stone spiral stair, which was added by JC Curwen who bought the house two years after Braithwaite built it. The National Trust now owns the building, which was generously given to them with much of the surounding area by local celebrity, Beatrix Potter.

There is another folly, which provides the motivation for a delightful half hours walk through the woods to Claife Heights above the Station cottage. It is quite difficult to find as it has lost its upper half and is now shielded by trees. The doorway has been bricked up and there is one simple plaque with a date, 1865 and the initials, R, S & F.

HAWKSHEAD

WORDSWORTH'S GRAFFITI

Location: Hawkshead Grammar School, opposite the main car park. SD3598

Access: Open April to October, Monday to Saturday, Sunday afternoons only and closed on Wednesdays.

Like most naughty school boys, William Wordsworth spent one rather boring lesson carving his name into his desk top, where it can still be seen today, especially as it now had a small glass covering.

The school was founded in 1585 by the Archbishop Edwin Sandys. On display inside you can see the original charter granted by Queen Elizabeth in 1588 for the school to teach 100 pupils. The building is so small it is difficult to imagine it could seat so many pupils, it is really just one classroom, which is still set out as it was in the late 18th century. There is a small library and a brief history of the school on the upper floor. The main school room has four sentences written on the walls in large lettering; the one in front of Wordsworth's desk reads: 'Books we know are a substantial world both pure and good.'

If you are on the Wordsworth trail, you will not be disappointed. Nearly everywhere you go in the Lake District you will come across somewhere where he lived, or died or visited.

HAWKSHEAD

THE HORSE TROUGH

Location:	Leave Hawkshead on the B5285, going north, take the first left turn and, after a couple of miles, the trough is on the left as you descend the hill to Coniston.

This elaborate horse trough was erected in 1885 as a memorial by Susanna Beever. An engraving on a stone slab recalls the days when we were dependent on horses for our transport, it reads:

A Righteous Man
Regards the life
of his Beast.

In the middle there is a drinking station for humans with the words 'keep the pavement dry' written on the cast iron panel above the makers name: T Kennedy, Patentee, Kilmarnock.

GRIZEDALE

GRIZEDALE FOREST SCULPTURES

Location: Between Lake Coniston and Windermere, signposted left just before Hawkshead, coming from the south. SD335944. There is an excellent Visitors' Centre here, with a good book shop and tea room. Also mountain bike hire with trail maps.

The Sculpture Project was established in 1977 to 'provide a working environment for sculptors . . . to create projects which vitally spring from their response to the forest'. The result is fascinating; as you walk round the forest you come across the sculptures quite unexpectedly, nestling in the undergrowth and hidden among the trees. One of my favourites is a tree hung with dozens of simple wooden chairs, which have now weathered and appear to have rejoined the tree from where they once came; a man made object returning to nature. The one pictured here is by David Kemp and is called Ancient Forester (1982–84)

Grizedale Forest is also famous for its 'Theatre in the Forest', which attracts international performers and musicians and an enthusiastic audience.

GRASMERE

WORDSWORTH'S GRAVE AT ST OSWALD'S CHURCH AND THE GINGERBREAD HOUSE

Location:	North of Ambleside on the A591. NY3407

The famous graves of the Wordsworth family are well-signposted and must be among the most visited tombstones in Britain.

THE GINGERBREAD HOUSE is a sweet little cottage right next door to the church Lych Gate which was originally the village school from 1660–1854. The famous Grasmere Gingerbread has been made here for 130 years.

THE ROCK OF NAMES

In the garden of Dove cottage, where Wordsworth lived, is a slab of stone on which has been carved a list of initials, including Wordsworth, his sister Dorothy and Coleridge, known as the Rock of Names. It once stood in a wood near the Straining Well above Legburthwaite, where a small commemorative plaque has been placed to mark the original spot.

Dove Cottage is now the Wordsworth Museum which illustrates the poet's life and works with manuscripts, portraits and memorabilia. It is open daily from 9.30am–5.30pm except from mid-January to mid-February and Christmas Day. The staff are extremely knowledgeable and helpful. There is also an excellent book shop and restaurant. Although Dove Cottage was originally an inn, Dorothy Wordwworth's hospitality only stretched to porridge, obliging her guests to sneak out of the window to find a decent meal elsewhere.

Rock of Names, Dove Cottage

Sarah Nelson's Grasmere Gingerbread

GRASMERE

POET'S WALK, A TRIBUTE TO DOROTHY WORDSWORTH

Location:	Take the Easedale road out of Grasmere until you get to the Lancrigg Vegetarian Country House Hotel. NY329086

This delightful hotel is in a wonderful situation with idyllic Lakeland views. Follow the footpath up behind the hotel and enter the woods. On the pathway stands a small rock with the following words inscribed on a plaque:

Hoc in
Supercilio Sedebat
Dorothea
Wordsworth
Dum Ex Ore Fratris
Prope inambulantis
Carmina Describit

This is a tribute to Dorothy Wordsworth, written by her famous brother, who bought this house on behalf of a female friend, and stayed here as a guest. On the stone he explains that this is the place where he gets his inspiration while his sister writes down his words. It was a popular spot for the poets who often sat in the 'therapeutic pools' in the river. There is a pair of graves in the woods of two beloved dogs, belonging to the lady of the house.

GRASMERE

UNUSUAL ROCK FORMATIONS

Location:	These unusual rock formations are on Helm Crag above Grasmere, north of Ambleside on the A591. NY326093. There are many wonderful walks in this area. Helm Crag is well-signposted from the Easeldale road in Grasmere. It is a 1,000ft climb but worth every step because of the magnificent views from the top.

Just outside the village of Grasmere, pull in to the Travellers Rest pub on the main road. If you look up to Helm Crag, which is the hill dominating the area, you will see a rock formation on the southern-most pinnacle known locally as the Lion and the Lamb. It can also be seen from the streets of Grasmere.

Further along the road as you ascend towards Dunmail Raise, look up to your left to see the northern pinnacle (and highest point) of Helm Crag, which is known as the Old Woman Playing an Organ. Listen carefully, as it is sometimes possible to hear her lonely tunes.

The Lion and the Lamb

The old woman playing an organ

THIRLMERE

THE WATERWORKS

Location: On the A591 between Ambleside and Keswick. NY3215

Access: No access, but can be seen in passing.

This is an extraordinary building right on the shore of Lake Thirlmere; it looks like a castle with its turrets, battlements and even a painted crest, but is actually the Manchester Corporation Waterworks.The scheme was sanctioned by the city council in 1877, authorised by an Act of Parliament(!) in 1879. The building was completed in1894. There is a large plaque on one side on which is listed the Chairmen and Deputy Chairmen of the council who were involved in the project. It starts with John Crave with his dates of office 1867–1880, and ends with Sir Cosdin Thomas Leech who was deputy Chairman in 1886, but whose end of posting is left mysteriously blank.

BORROWDALE

THE BOWDER STONE

Location:	South of Keswick on the B5289, half way up the Borrowdale valley, the 600m pathway is well-signposted. NY255164

This is an impressive 30ft-high stone weighing 1900 tons which defies gravity. It is one of the most famous features in the Lake District; technically it is called a 'Glacial Erratic' and was carried down the valley by a glacier during the last ice age. As the ice melted, this rock was left high and dry, precariously balanced on a knife edge. You can even shake someone's hand beneath the stone through a gap at its base. A ladder allows you to climb to the top to appreciate the stunning views. The overhanging side of the stone is also popular with local rock climbers.

KESWICK

THE ONE-HANDED CLOCK

Location:	On the A66, which runs east west across the top of the Lake District. NY2723

Right in the centre of this busy town, stands a tower with an unusual clock, it only has one hand. If you look closely, you can see the other hand, but it is painted black so cannot be seen against the background. You may wonder why! The clock, bell and materials were taken from Lord's Island on Derwent Water and reassembled here.

Around 1571 the building on this site was used as a court house and prison. It was rebuilt in1695, then again in 1813.

KESWICK

THE CUMBERLAND PENCIL COMPANY

Location: On the A66, which runs east west across the top of the Lake District.

Access: Open all year, all week,˙ (9.30am–4pm).

The 1930s factory is right next door to a museum, which takes you through the process from mining the graphite in Borrowdale to the final details of making this famous brand of pencil. It also houses the world's largest pencil, which is recorded in the Guinness Book of Records. Local supplies are delivered in this old van, creating a romantic nostalgia of our school days.

A row of coloured pencils make up the fence either side of the bus stop outside Frizington Library on the road from Egremont to Cockermouth.

CASTLERIGG

THE STONE CIRCLE

Location:	One mile east of Keswick, off the A66. NY2822

The Castlerigg Stone Circle is also known as the Keswick Carles and was built around 2000BC, in the 'Neolithic Age'. These ceremonial stones stand in a circle on open fell ground, with a stunning panorama across Helvellyn and the hills of the northern lakes. There are 38 stones with a further ten set in a rectangle 'sanctuary' in the middle of the circle. No-one knows exactly why the stones were placed here, but there has been a suggestion that local tribal communities came here to exchange partners! There is also some evidence to suggest that farmers used the circle to calculate the cycle of the seasons. They are made of Borrowdale volcanic rock, brought by glaciers from rocky outcrops during the last ice age.

The Circle is managed by English Heritage and has been owned since 1913 by the National Trust. It was one of the first dozen sites to be declared an ancient monument. An informative notice-board at the entrance to the site gives the background and history of the Circle.

COCKERMOUTH

THE BUTTER BELL

Location: 7 Market Place, Cockermouth. NY1230

This historic Butter Bell used to be rung on market days. Nowadays it looks very odd, embedded in the bright yellow wall of a Chinese Take away shop! Don't miss the annual Cockermouth festival during the third week in August, when Cattle and Sheep Auctions, concerts and exhibitions take place.

Also in Cockermouth, in the car park next to the information centre, is a plaque on a small stone stump. It reads:

On 17th May 1568
There came to this house
as a guest of Henry Fletcher Esq
Mary Queen of Scotts
On her journey from
Workington to Carlisle.

EAGLESFIELD, COCKERMOUTH

FLETCHER CHRISTIAN'S BIRTHPLACE

Location:	At Eaglesfield, at Moorland Close Farm, just outside of Cockermouth. Turn left after the school, then next left again up an unmetalled bridle way. NY1230

Fletcher Christian was born here in 1764. He was the ringleader of the mutiny against Captain William Bligh on the Bounty in 1789. Bligh and Christian were good friends and had sailed on many voyages together, mostly to the West Indies. The Bounty was on a trip to Tahiti to collect bread-fruits, which went disastrously wrong. Christian initiated a mutiny in a story made famous by the movie, in which Marlon Brando starred alongside Trevor Howard. Christian and eight other mutineers took refuge on Pitcairn Island and founded a settlement with some Tahitians. He never again returned to this little hamlet in the corner of the Lake District where he grew up and went to school.

Fletcher Christian has a well-known descendent; the cookery broadcaster Glynn Christian, who has recently led a discovery expedition to the West Indies and has written an excellent book on the subject.

The plaque stands on a wall in the yard of Moorland Close farm. The Latin inscription reads: *Salus per Christum.*

You can see various items connected with Fletcher Christian in the Maryport Maritime Museum. (Next to the quay, open all year, except Sunday and Wednesday, admission free).

EAGLESFIELD

THE DALTON PLAQUE

Location:	In the village of Eaglesfield, just outside of Cockermouth. NY1230

In this insignificant hamlet, a man was born who made a very significant discovery which made an enormous difference to our world. Above an old wooden door on a small white-painted house, reads this inscription:

John Dalton DCL LLD
the discoverer of
The Atomic Theory
Was born here 5th September 1766
Died at Manchester 27th July 1844

Not far away, is Sellafield (née Windscale) the Atomic Energy plant which is now open to the public.

HIGH LORTON

THE OLD SMOKE HOUSE

Location:	On the B5292, south from Cockermouth. NY1625

In the 19th century, ham and fish used to be cured over an oak fire in this round stone tower. It has an iron framed roof and is a Grade II listed building. The smoke house holds a special place in the hearts of local people, which has recently been lovingly restored with a restoration grant from the National Park . . .

GREYSTOKE

FARMHOUSE FOLLIES

Location: North of the A66 between Greystoke and Penrith on the B5288. NY4530

Access: No public access, but they can all be clearly seen from the road.

The Greystoke Estates are famous as the birthplace of Tarzan, and are said to be the largest area of private land not crossed by public roads or paths. The Duke of Norfolk was an eccentric folly builder who must have had a brilliant sense of humour. He lived at Greystoke Castle, and is said to have built these follies to annoy his Tory neighbour, the Earl of Lonsdale from Lowther Castle. He was a Whig Aristocrat, and gave names to the Estate farms which were associated with the American War of Independence.

FORT PUTNAM

It is difficult to believe that this is just a working farm, as the functional outbuildings are surrounded by a grand fortified wall, complete with castellations and hexagonal watchtower. The cow house is made up of a row of Gothic-style arches and pillars, which are adorned with crowns of stone petals. The farm was originally called Mount Putnam, and was named after General Israel 'Puffing' Putnam.

Fort Putnam Farm

BUNKERS HILL

This farm has a castle-style wall on three sides with Gothic pointed windows. Another farm nearby is called Jefferson, with obvious American connections, although it is unusual in name only.

GREYSTOKE

THE COTTAGE BUILT TO LOOK LIKE A CHURCH

Location: The Spire House, north of the A66, between Greystoke and Penrith. NY462313

Access: No access as it is still a private farm.

From a distance you can see the spire, down a lane parallel with the Greystoke road, and are fooled into thinking that it is a church. As you approach, you realise that the spire is only three sided and has been attached to the front of a modest farm house. You get a real shock when you walk round the back; it's a row of cow sheds!

The story goes of how the local farmer told the Duke that his 'creed did not necessitate church attendance for worship and that his own house would suffice'. The Duke took him at his word and built a farmhouse that looked like a church! There is another story, that Charles Howard, aka the Duke, commissioned his architect to build anything 'as long as it didn't look like a church'. Surely he must have got the sack . . .

Not much is known about the architect of all these wonderful 200-year-old follies, but it is thought that Francis Horne, who was staying at Greystoke in 1787 was probably responsible. He was involved in various projects with the 11th Duke, including the alterations to Arundel Castle and the folly Horne's Tower. However, it is also thought that the Duke himself could have been the architect, and Francis Horne's role was simply an advisory one.

DACRE

THE CAT-EATING BEARS

Location:	At St Andrew's Church, off the A66, south west of Penrith. NY460266

In the four corners of the graveyard of this delightful little church, you will find the most extraordinary stone monuments; four bears in various stages of eating a cat. Unfortunately the features have been eroded by the weather over the years.

Also in Dacre is a small castle, which can be admired from the church.

ULLSWATER

LYULPH'S TOWER

Location:	On the A592; in the National Trust's Gowbarrow Park on the west side of Ullswater. NY403204
Access:	No access but it can be seen from the road.

This 3-sided castellated 'folly' with octagonal turrets on each corner was built in 1780 by the 11th Duke of Norfolk, as a hunting lodge for shooting picnics. It is said to have been named after the legendary Saxon hero Lyulph. However, there is another theory concerning the origin of the name; Baron de L'Ulf of Greystoke who was the first Baron of Ullswater was thought to have lived here in a medieval tower.

Lyulph's Tower is known as the first 'picturesque' house in the area, which was popular in the 18th century. Ullswater is famous for it sextuple echo, a feature which was exploited to the full by the Duke of Portland 'who kept a boat on the lake with brass guns, for the purpose of exciting echoes'.

Lyulph's Tower is situated in Gowbarrow Park which is covered with daffodills during the spring and inspired Wordsworth's most famous poem. In 1802, Wordsworth is said to have walked through the park with Dorothy on his way to visit the Clarksons, who lived at Eusemere near Pooley Bridge. The Park is owned by the National Trust.

PENRITH

STREET SIGNS

Location: Town Centre. NY5130

THE LAMB

There is a sweet little lamb stuck to the wall over the arched gateway to Crown Terrace, just off King Street. It is dated 1776. This building used to be the Wool merchants Hall when Penrith was in its heyday and wool was an important commodity.

THE SADDLERS ON LITTLE DOCKRAY

This shop used to have a white horse's head on the wall, but when the owner died, it was assumed the business would no longer be continued, so it was sold off to a local jockey. However, the shop is still a thriving saddlery business, (selling 'bridal' wear, according to a misspelling in a newspaper advert.) The current owner has just commissioned a new horse's head to display over his doorway to continue the tradition which was once a familiar site. Round the back of the building there is an inscription with a date and a pair of saddle scissors.

PENRITH

THE GIANT'S THUMB AND THE RAILWAY MONUMENT

Location:	St Andrew's Church, town centre NY5130

THE GIANT'S THUMB is a Saxon cross which has been in this churchyard since 920AD, a generation before the 'Giant's Grave'. It is amazing to think that a church has stood on this site for over 1500 years, when St Ninian first brought Christianity to this region.

THE RAILWAY MONUMENT is a tall, rectangular 'gothic' style monument erected in memory of the Superintendent of the construction of the Carlisle to Lancaster Railway in 1844.

The Railway Monument

The Giant's Thumb

PENRITH

THE GIANT'S GRAVE.

Location:	At St Andrew's Church, town centre of Penrith, Junction 40 off the M6, at the A66/A6. NY5130

Ewan Caesarius, King of Cumbria from 900–937AD was once thought to be the giant buried in this church. 'Owen the Great' as he was also known, used to rule Cumbria when Penrith was a place of great significance. The 'grave' is not one monument but is made up by two ancient crosses fifteen feet apart with four 'hog back' tombstones in the middle. The South West one has the figure of a priest on one end, but it is now difficult to make it out. They have been dated from about 950–1000AD and are carved with faded patterns. Details of the history can be found on the wall just inside the main entrance of the church.

PENRITH

THE TOWN GALLOWS

Location:	At the Cross Keys Pub in Carleton, on the A686, 1 mile north east of Penrith. NY532298

Set in the barn wall of this 17th-century pub, is the town gallows, or more technically, the gibbet. This is the name of a gallows put up near the scene of the crime on which the criminal was suspended in chains after his execution. Fortunately this grim practice was abolished in 1834.

One criminal whose 'body was left to hang until all the flesh was rotted away and only the skeleton remained' was Thomas Nicholson, and now thought to haunt the Pub. The full story is displayed on the walls of the Bar, along with the history of the building and local folklore.

EAMONT BRIDGE, PENRITH

MAYBURGH HENGE AND KING ARTHUR'S ROUND TABLE

Location: At Eamont Bridge just south of Penrith on the A6. NY519284

A henge is a circular earthwork with one or more entrances surrounding an area about 120 metres across. The Mayburgh henge is an outstanding example of Neolithic activity in Cumbria. In the middle of a large 'crater' on this raised ground, lies a single 'standing stone' or monolith, which dates from about 2000BC. In the 18th century there were at least eight other stones.

A quarter of a mile away to the east is KING ARTHUR'S ROUND TABLE and one of England's best henges. It is less obvious than the Mayburgh one. We still do not know what function or purpose these places held in Neolithic society, but it is assumed that they were used as temples whose 'banks and ditches defined the sacred area within' or as a meeting place for a large prehistoric community.

EAMONT BRIDGE, PENRITH

SOLDIER'S FACES ON A MEMORIAL

Location: A few miles south of Penrith on the A6. NY524284

This war memorial is unusual because it commemorates only two dead men and has their faces cast in iron mounted on the cross. The plaque reads:

'At that crisis in the history of the Empire when volunteers were invited for active service in the South African War, this village of Eamont Bridge sent four, John Hindson, William Todd, and Arthur Warwick of the 24th Company (Westmorland & Cumberland) Imperial Yeomanry, and William Hindson of the Volunteer Company of the Border regiment. Of these John Hindson and William Todd were killed in action at Fabers Put, 30th May 1900.'

The monument was put up with money raised by members of the village, on this historic site granted by Lord Brougham in 1906

BROUGHAM, NEAR PENRITH

THE CHINESE DOOR KNOCKER

Location: At Brougham Hall, 2 miles South east of Penrith off the A6. NY5328

In 1140AD a monk from Durham cathedral designed this unusual medieval sculpture door knocker. It was one of four, the others were made of bronze and are still in the Cathedral. Brougham Hall had a cast iron one which hung on the Great West Door until 1952, but then it disappeared. Twenty years later, a local businessman remembers being asked to parcel it up and send it to a London Auction house, not realising it had been stolen. During the restoration of the Hall, permission was sought from Durham Cathedral to make a cast copy replacement, but it was denied. So in 1993, a Bronze founder was discovered in Sussex who was able to make a copy from photographs.

Brougham (pronounced Broom) Hall was the 19th-century home of the Lord Chancellor of England, when it was known as the 'Windsor of the North'. It has been derelict since the 1930s but has now been rescued to provide a home for various traditional local crafts, such as masonry, slating, smithies and foundries. An interesting appeal has been set up to promote these disappearing skills in an area with 30% unemployment.

Nearby Brougham Castle stands on the banks of the River Eamont, and is also just a ruin, now managed by the English Heritage. It had a strategic importance with Brough Castle to defend the Pennines from York to Carlisle.

Lady Anne Clifford lived here in the 17th century, and was responsible for a significant restoration programme. There is an exhibition of Roman tombstones from the nearby fort. (Access: from April to September every day, from October to March open Wednesday to Sunday 10am–4pm)

BROUGHAM, NR PENRITH

THE COUNTESS PILLAR

Location:	On the A66, east of Penrith, next to Brougham Castle. NY548290

Lady Anne Clifford was an eccentric woman who lived in Brougham Castle in the 17th century. The pillar was put up in 1656 and commemorates her final parting with her 'good and pious' mother forty years before. The column has sundials on three sides, painted a vibrant blue and gold, and two carved coats of arms with a skull on the other.

On the south side there is an inscription requesting that an annuity of four pounds is to be distributed to the poor of the parish. This tradition is carried out during an annual ceremony to this day.

CLIFTON

THE FARMYARD TOWER

Location:	In the middle of a farmyard at Clifton, on the A6 South of Penrith. NY5326

The history of Clifton Hall is a sad one and the Tower is all that is left to show of it. Gilbert d'Engaine lived in the manor of Clifton from 1173 and was a prominent member of the Westmorland gentry. His descendants lived here for hundreds of years until it passed through marriage to the Wyberghs. In the middle of the seventeenth century the family fell into debt and lost their lands to a neighbour, Sir John Lowther, to whom the Hall was later sold.

The farm which surrounds the tower was built in the early part of the last century. English Heritage have looked after the site since 1973.

SHAP WELLS

QUEEN VICTORIA'S MONUMENT

Location: A few miles south east of Shap, off the A6. (J 39 off M6) Shap Wells has been a hotel since 1833, and is now the largest family owned hotel in Cumbria. It is way off the beaten track and an ideal base from which to explore the numerous attractions in the area.

The 23ft-high column has stood on a hill near the hotel since June 1842. It has a 6ft statue of Britannia on the top with inscriptions and bas relief carvings round the base. The monument was commissioned by William Lowther, the Earl of Lonsdale 'to commemorate the Accession of Queen Victoria to the Throne of these Realms, June 20th 1837'.

It was designed by a Mr Mawson and has the Lowther Estate arms on the north side; a wreath of palm and olive which represent peace and plenty. On the west side there is a bas relief of the British lion resting his paw on the globe. On the east side is a figure of the Goddess Hygeia, pouring medicinal waters from a goblet into a shell.

Thomas Bland of Reagill is the artist responsible for these wonderful sculptures and carvings.

An excellent booklet on the local history of the hotel is available at the reception, including the period of the Second World War, when the hotel was used as a prisoner of war camp for German officers (including a fascinating 'great escape' story). Apparently even Rudolph Hess was imprisoned here, providing quite a contrast to the hotel's previous most famous visitor; Queen Victoria's Aunt, the Countess of Harewood.

SHAP WELLS

THE WELL HEAD

Location:	In the woods next to Shap Wells Hotel, off the A6 south of Penrith. NY5713

Shap Wells used to be a very popular place for the 'nobility, Gentry and public' to bathe in or drink the waters of the Spa well, which were thought to contain curative properties. They are no longer in use, but the covered well head can still be seen. The mineral water used to contain calcium,chloride and sodium chloride with some Epsom salts,and apparently smelt like rotten eggs! It can still be sampled from a spring on the river bank, but it is not recommended.

According to a fascinating booklet available from the hotel, it was a primitive place in those days. The following description appeared in 'A hand book to the Shap Spa', published in 1844.

'The building resembled an old peat-cote: within a rusty iron pot or boiler, heated when required (but often not) with turf, whins (gorse) and heather, and the bath tank an old hogshead. When a bath was required, the patient had to wait, be the weather what it might, till all was ready; he then scrambled in to the hogshead.'

SHAP

THE ABBEY IN THE FARMYARD

Location:	One mile west of Shap off the A6, south of Penrith. NY547154

Most towers, ruins and follies in this book are quite easy to find as they were usually built on the top of a hill. The Abbey of St Mary on the other hand, is completely hidden at the bottom of a steep valley, on the banks of the River Lowther. The extraordinary thing about the Abbey now, is its location in the middle of a farm yard. Apparently some of the stones were removed from the abbey and can now be seen in the walls of Lowther Castle.

Only one 16th-century tower of this Premonstratensian Abbey is still standing. It was inhabited by an order of regular canons founded by St Norbert at Prémontré in France in 1119. The monks were called 'the white monks' because of their white habits, and combined a life of prayer with local community work.

After the Disssolution in 1540, the Abbot and his Canons were pensioned off, the Abbey's extensive lands were sold , some of the buildings were converted for farm use and the rest was allowed to decay.

REAGILL

GARDEN SCULPTURES

Location: Three miles north east of Shap, across the motorway going towards Sleagill. NY607108

To the east side of the M6 motorway is a quiet part of rural England, undisturbed by tourists or the twentieth century. You follow a maze of country lanes through farm lands to the little village of Reagill, where Thomas Bland, the self taught sculptor lived. William Lowther, the Earl of Lonsdale of Lowther Castle was a great man for using local talent in his architectural projects and commissioned Bland to work on the Victoria Monument at Shap Wells. Examples of his other work can be seen in this modest farmhouse garden, which is full of stone animals, fairy figures, and kings and queens.

GREAT SALKELD

THE REARING RAM GATEPOSTS

Location:	At the entrance to Nunwick Hall on the B6412 above the A686, north east of Penrith. NY555364

A pair of rearing Rams each holding the family coat of arms stand at the entrance to this red sandstone private house, which can be seen on the main road going north from Long Meg. The house was acquired by Richard Heywood Thompson in 1890.

LITTLE SALKELD

LONG MEG AND HER DAUGHTERS

Location:	Near Little Salkeld, off the A686, 6 miles north east of Penrith

This is one of the best-preserved examples of a Stone Circle.

Long Meg is the name of a 15ft-high stone standing alone outside the main circle, which is made up of her 65 'daughters'. There were originally about 70 stones, made of New Red Sandstone. The cup and ring symbols which adorn Long Meg are thought to have been carved over 4000 years ago!

According to local legend , Long Meg was a witch who turned to stone with her daughters for 'profaning the Sabbath with wild dancing'. It is said that Long Meg is a magic circle and that if you manage to count the same number of stones twice, then Long Meg will come to life or the Devil himself will appear! The stone was possibly named after a real witch, Meg of Malden, who lived in the 17th century.

LITTLE SALKELD WATERMILL

The word Salkeld is from the Norse language and means 'the spring among the willows', proving that they had much more imagination in the olden days! Just down the road at Little Salkeld is the 18th-century Watermill, which is one of the country's few working waterpowered mills still producing organic flour the traditional way. You can see the two 12ft cast-iron waterwheels and it also has an excellent tea shop!

KIRKOSWALD

THE VICAR'S TOWER AND THE NUNNERY

Location:	On the B6412 above the A686, north east of Penrith. SD5540

The word 'kirk' comes from the Norse and means 'church', which crops up all over Cumbria. This grand monument stands on a hill overlooking the delightful village of Kirkoswold on one side and the church on the other. There is a weather vane on the top of the building which has the date 1743 punched out of it. The inscription reads:

This tower was rebuilt
AD1893
In memory of
John Henry Ransome
Vicar 1877–1892

THE NUNNERY is one mile up out of the village, and is now a country house hotel where you can get a good cup of tea or ice cream. The Nunnery Walks can be started from here, which take in some wonderful scenery through ancient woods and along the banks of the River Eden. In front of the house a sign explains:

Over 200 years ago walks were created as part of a fashionable desire to improve on nature and create romantic landscapes . . .

The walks were formed by Christopher Aglionby, whose family swopped the Nunnery in 1696 for Drumburgh Castle with Sir John Lowther. The Gothic stables are dated 1827 and are said to be haunted.

CALDBECK

THE GRAVES OF JOHN PEEL AND THE MAID OF BUTTERMERE

Location: In Caldbeck Church, on the B5299, South West of Carlisle. NY3339

John Peel was a living legend made famous with the song 'D'ye ken John Peel', which was written after his death in 1854. He was born in 1777 and spent his life as a passionate huntsman. Nowadays, his tombstone is often the target of anti-bloodsports vandals.

Mary Robinson was the beautiful daughter of a local landlord, who became famous when Wordsworth wrote a poem about her. She was unfortunate to marry a real rogue, who already had two wives. In 1803 he was arrested and hanged for forgery and Mary became the subject of much sympathy and attention, whose popularity has not eased with time; Melvyn Bragg has recently written a novel about her.

CURTHWAITE

A HOUSE IN THE SHAPE OF A FIDDLE

Location:	At Fiddleback Farmhouse, outside the village of Curthwaite on the A595, south of Thursby. NY3040

A very curious cottage built in 1709 to resemble the shape of a fiddle or a figure-of-eight. Over the entrance is a curved decoration rather like a musical note.

A hundred yards from the farm is a splendid archway which one assumes is the entrance to a grand Estate, but it is just a country road, signposted to Crofton.

WETHERAL

THE GATEWAY TO NOWHERE AND THE CHURCH WINDOW IN A GARDEN

Location:	South east of Carlisle on the B6263. NY4855

This tower is now a gatehouse leading to nowhere. It has had an interesting history, ranging from great importance as a Benedictine Priory in an age when religion was everything, to the lowly function as a common hayloft. It now stands as a lonely curiosity, overlooking the River Eden and visited only by the occasional tourist.

The Priory was dedicated to the Holy Trinity and St Constantine and was founded in 1106. The 15th-century Gatehouse was once the entrance to the monastic outer court, in which many grand buildings would have stood, including a chapel, administrative offices and a monastic school. It has now been beautifully restored by Engish Heritage. It is possible to climb up the spiral staircase inside to view the 'domestic chambers' (bedrooms to you and me) above the entrance hall, which were used by either a Priory official or by visitors and travellers.

THE CHURCH WINDOW IN A GARDEN

Whoof House, near Wetheral, on the A69, is a large house which has now been converted into several dwellings, with a modern extension on the back providing a strange juxtaposition with history. A large gothic church window stands in the garden leaning against the modern brickwork. It was transported here in 1868 from Arthureth Church in Aglionby near Longtown.

CORBY

SLEEPING DOGS AND A VULCAN'S FORGE

Location: In the village of Corby, South East of Carlisle off the B6263

Over the door way of Grove Cottage lie two sweet little dogs, forever sleeping in the sun.

In the central cross-roads of the village, you can't miss the impressive arch with its grand pillars, which is used as a garage these days. It was built as the smithy in the image of a Vulcan's Forge.

The Statue of St Constantine dressed in a monk's heavy robes with crossed swords at his feet, he is staring out across the river, at the cell in which he lived at Wetheral (NY4655). He was placed on the river bank by Henry Howard in 1833 opposite 'St Constantine's cells' which were medieval caves used as hermitages.

CORBY

THE HOWARD LION AND THE CORBY CASCADE

The Castle is built of red sandstone and originally was just a pele tower. The Howard Lion stands proudly on the roof top. It used to be fashionable to have romantic ruins and grottoes on your estate and there are many curious surprises in the grounds which can be viewed during a pleasant stroll.

THE CORBY CASCADE is a wonderful architectural extravagance straight out of Italy, where the builder Thomas Howard was obviously inspired. High on the river bank stands an open-sided temple containing a statue of Neptune and stone carvings of mermaids. The water used to rush right through the middle of it from a tunnel behind, out through the open jaws of a monster and between two Hounds of Hades, then drop 100 feet to the lower steps through another archway, past a statue of Nelson and out to the river Eden.

WREAY

THE GARDEN-SHED CHAPEL

Location:	Between the M6 and A6, South of Carlisle. NY4449

Miss Sarah Losh is the surprising architect of various buildings in Wreay, not least because she was a woman. In 1817 she went on the Grand Tour ending up in Naples, and on her return home started practising as an architect. In 1830 she built the village school and the school master's house, which was based on the measurements of an 1800-year-old house she had seen in Pompei. She built the Mortuary Chapel next to the churchyard, which is now used as a garden shed! It is a replica of St Perran's Oratory, excavated in Cornwall in 1835, from which she made accurate drawings. Ms Losh also designed a Tudor house at Langarth, the wellhead at St Ninian's in Brisco and the Sexton's cottage next to the churchyard.

WREAY

ST MARY'S CHURCH

Sarah Losh's greatest achievement, however, is the Church. It has her individuality stamped all over it and includes many unusual stone and wood carvings. Inside there are two huge wooden lecterns of an eagle and a flapping pelican, interesting furniture,and a carved font and pulpit. Wooden pine cones feature as door handles and on pillars, which are in memory of Major William Thain, a friend who was shot by a poisoned arrow in the Khyber Pass. He had once sent her a cone from which she grew a tree. Outside, the walls are decorated with a stone serpent, a bat, dragon gargoyles, a crocodile and a turtle (pictured below).

CARLISLE

MISERICORDS IN THE CATHEDRAL

Location: In Carlisle Cathedral, J43 off the M6, or A6. NY4056

Access: Open daily, 7.30am–6.30pm. Guides available.

These 46 misericords are the medieval carvings which adorn the underside of the 15th-century choir stalls. They are more of a perch than a seat, which banged down with a clatter if the Monk should dare to fall asleep. Nothing is known about the carver but he obviously had a free reign with his subject matter. The symbolic images are mostly of Dragons, Griffins and Angels.

The one pictured here is the 'Mayor Wyvern'; an evil creature which represents the devil and could kill with the whiplash from its tail. External evil is represented by lumps on its back, strong eagle like legs and bat-like wings which signify darkness. The use of a cold-blooded body of a serpent and the warm-blooded head of a beast represented internal evil. The Wyvern is flanked by two lions with human heads.

There is an excellent booklet with all the weird and wonderful stories behind these carvings, written and illustrated by Thirlie Grundy and available in the Cathedral book shop.

On the wall outside the main entrance of the Cathedral, is a gargoyle with a remarkable resemblance to Scooby Doo.

Carlisle Castle is just a few minutes walk away and definitely worth a look round. The 12th-century keep and Queen Mary's tower (where she was imprisoned in 1568) are interesting, and also the dungeon containing the 'licking stone'. Open daily, year round.

CARLISLE

THE CARLISLE CROSS AND THE TOLL GATEWAY TO THE CITY

Location: Junction 43 off the M6, or take the A6 north from Penrith. NY4056

The market cross or 'Carel Cross' was put up in 1682 by Mayor Joseph Reed in the centre of Carlisle. On the top are four sundials and a lion resting his paw on the Dormont Book of the city.

The city is entered through a red stone arch, which has an interesting board displaying the tolls payable on certain goods. Grain is charged at 1d per cart load, 'earthenware, hardware, guano and all artificial manures' is under 1d per horse cart load. It cost 4d to take cattle and sheep into the city, except during the annual fair in August when it cost double.

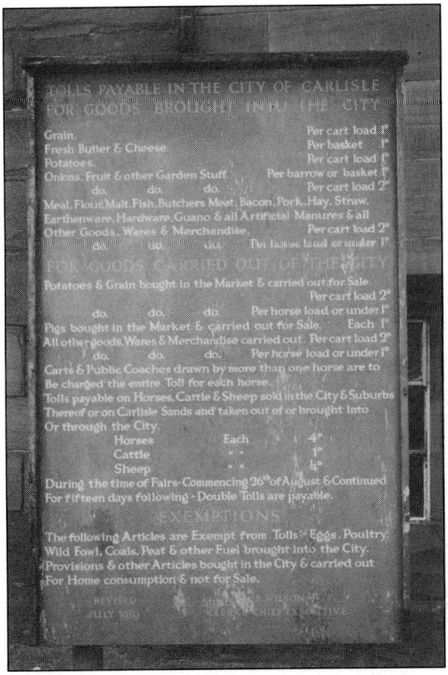

Unbelievably, the sign was revised as recently as July 1979 by R. Wilson, Clerk and Chief Executive.

Carlisle hosts the annual Cumberland Agricultural fair in July, and the revived Carlisle Great Fair in August.

CARLISLE

THE CITADEL OR COURT HOUSES

The Citadel towers served as part of the defences of the city, in addition to Carlisle Castle. They were built in 1810 from an original design by Thomas Telford to replace the original towers which were built on the orders of Henry VIII in 1542. The towers once enclosed an area of 37 acres and were connected by a medieval wall, which can still be seen on the west side.

THE STATION

Above the entrance of the station are three coats of arms. At one time the railway here was managed by seven different companies; the coats of Arms of the Lancaster & Carlisle Co and the Caledonian company line are all that remain.

Just across from the Station is the old Gaol wall, which was the site of the last public execution in Carlisle on the 15th March 1862. A commemorative plaque has been put up by the civic trust.

BRAMPTON

THE MARKET CROSS

Location:	On the A69 north east of Carlisle.

This elaborate octagonal market cross is known as the Howard Memorial Shelter and stands in the central square of Brampton, itself a crossing point for all the roads in the area, which still hosts a market once a week. The building is now the Tourist Information Office, but was built to commemorate George James Howard of Naworth Park, 9th Earl of Carlisle who died in 1911 and his wife Rosalind Frances who died 1921. The Howards were supporters of the Temperance movement, and are chiefly remembered now as the ones who shut all the pubs in the area!

BEWCASTLE

THE 7TH-CENTURY CROSS

Location:	North West of Carlisle off the B6318

Bewcastle is now a bleak and isolated corner of the county, but it once was very important. It is quite extraordinary that this magnificent monument from the seventh century is located here. It is said that the cross is the greatest achievement of its date in the whole of Europe. The yellow sandstone cross stands nearly 15ft high and is carved with scrolls, knot work and images of religious figures, birds and beasts.

No-one knows exactly when the head of the Anglian cross fell off, but it is possible it went to London to the historian Camden in the early 1600s.

There is a very informative booklet on the history of the cross available in the church, and also a fascinating display in an annex building. The ruins of Bewcastle Castle stand adjacent.

APPLEBY IN WESTMORLAND

THE TAP HOUSE

Location:	12 miles south of Penrith on the A66, follow signs to Flakebridge from the station at Appleby. SD6822

This wonderful housing for a tap is an unusual feature and can be found in the middle of a wood, outside Flakebridge cottage. There are many delightful walks in the area following public footpaths, see O.S. map Landranger 97.

Appleby is the county town of Westmorland and is famous for its annual horse fair in June. Appleby Castle is right in the middle of the town and is open to the public in the summer. It has an 11th-century keep, an art gallery and a wildlife conservation centre.

KIRKBY STEPHEN

FANCY LYCH-GATE

Location:	South of Brough on the A685. SD780509

A lych-gate is the roofed gateway to a churchyard where the coffin was rested, because it was considered unlucky to bring the body into the church before the ceremony had started. Most lych-gates are dull wooden affairs, but the one at Kirkby Stephen is very grand indeed. It has a large colonnaded entrance complete with a bell, a globe and a cross on top. The whole thing is painted bright pink The inscription on the stone portico reads:

Built by direction of the will of John Waller Esq.
a Purser in his Majesty's Navy and a Native of this town, 1810.
George Gibson, Architect and William Richardson, mason.

SEDBERGH

BONNIE PRINCE CHARLIE'S CHIMNEY

Location:	Weaver's yard in the town centre, on the A684 east of Kendal and the M6, towards Hawes. SD6591

Down an alley way off the main street, is Weaver's yard where you can see the chimney in which Bonnie Prince Charlie is said to have been hidden. Charles Edward Stuart came from Scotland to take over the English throne, but the English had other ideas and set out to kill him. The English and the Scots had a battle on Clifton Moor, which is just south of Penrith, and Bonnie Prince Charlie fled in disguise as a woman to the Isle of Skye. He was eventually captured in Carlisle in 1745.

The chimney is wide enough to 'roast an ox', and could easily have accomodated a man. Unfortunately the chemist who now owns the building, one of the oldest in Sedbergh, will not allow visitors and told me that Bonnie Prince Charlie is supposed to have taken refuge is dozens of houses in the area!

If you stroll up the main street, there's a very good chance that you will encounter Lester, singing ballads and recounting the history of Sedbergh. He gave me a guided tour including showing me an image of Bonnie Prince Charlie scratched into the wall next to the Cannon house. He lives in a hut which he calls the 'heartbreak hotel' and said he was not a poacher, but a gamekeeper; meaning that the game he found, he kept.

SEDBERGH

THE CANNONS SET IN CONCRETE

Location:	Outside Cannon House, in the town centre of Sedbergh. NY6591

Cannon house is on the street facing the Sedbergh school playing fields. Curiously, there are two small cannons embedded into the pavement tarmac next to a drainpipe outside this modest white washed house. They could not be of much use to anyone at their present angle, as they are pointing skywards. The cannons date from the Jacobite Rebellion of 1745 and the house was said to have been a haven for escaping rebels, although two cannons parked outside must surely have given the game away.

DENT

THE DRINKING FOUNTAIN

Location:	South of Sedbergh, off the A683/4. SD700808

This is one of the most delightful villages in the county, all cobbledy streets, higglety pigglety with pubs and rosy cottages. Over a hundred years ago the poet Coleridge immortalised this village, which was once a large and prosperous town.

The Drinking Fountain is set in a solid block of local Granite at the point where three streets meet in the centre of Dent. It was built to commemorate Adam Sedgewick 1785–1873, a local boy made good, who went to the local grammar school and then to nearby Sedbergh Public School. He later became a famous geologist, making many discoveries about the earth's crust, details of which can be seen in the Geology Museum in South Kensington. It's functional purpose is to quench the thirst of travellers, but it also provides some prankish amusement after the pubs have shut (according to the guy who lives in the house behind the fountain).

Just outside Dent is a series of waterfalls on the River Dee, including one spot called Hell's Cauldron, where water gushes over the Limestone rocks and tumbles into a black abyss. Also outside of Dent is the railway station. This is the highest mainline station in England (1136ft), and is part of the famous Carlisle to Settle line which has recently been rescued from closure after a long campaign.

MIDDLETON

THE ROMAN MILESTONE

Location:	Between Kirkby Lonsdale and Sedbergh on the A683. SD620858

In the field overlooking the church stands a four foot high stone column which has stood here since the Roman times. It bears a latin inscription and a date. The Romans arrived in Britain in 43AD and by 78AD Julius Agricola had established a whole network of roads, communications and fortifications all over England and right up to Scotland.The Middleton Milestone marks a point on this important route, which ran between Ribchester and Carlisle enabling troops to move quickly to meet the hostile Picts from the North.

KIRKBY LONSDALE

THE DEVIL'S BRIDGE AND THE CRAFTY CRONE OF KIRKBY

Location:	Off the A65, between the M6 (J36) and Settle. SD6178

This is one of the most famous bridges in the north of England and probably dates from late fourteenth century. There are several stories which attempt to explain where this bridge got its name, but the most popular legend is based on a poem, and concerns the Crafty Crone of Kirkby. The old woman lived beside the river, grazing her cattle on the other side, but after heavy rains she could not wade across the water as usual. The devil stepped in to offer her a deal; he would build her a bridge if she gave him the soul of the first creature who crossed it. As the story goes, the Devil built the bridge, then waited for her to cross it and therefore take her soul. However, the Crafty Crone threw a bun across the bridge, and her dog fetched it, thus forfeiting his soul.

It is interesting to note, that in fact, the bridge had more connection with God than the Devil, when a Vicar was granted permission in 1365 to levy a toll on travellers wishing to cross the bridge.

St Mary's Church in Kirkby Lonsdale is interesting. Between the Wars, the Church Font was used as a cattle trough by a local farm, but has now been restored to its rightful place. There is a gazebo in the church grounds with a fantastic view across the River Lune.

PUB SIGNS

The Lake District has numerous interesting and historical pubs, many with interesting signs:

THE MORTAL MAN

This curious sign can be seen swinging outside the Mortal Man pub in Troutbeck, north west of Windermere on the A592; a delightful country pub in a typical Lake District setting.

Oh mortal man that lives by bread,
What is it makes thy nose so red?
Thou silly fool that lookst so pale,
Tis drinking Sally Birketts ale

THE BEE HOUSE

You will find this one on the A6 just south of Penrith. There are a couple of bees buzzing around the sign, which has the following verse written on it:

In this Hive we are all Alive,
Good Liquor makes us funny
if you be dry step in and try,
The Virtue of our Honey

A CURIOSITY CONUNDRUM

And as the windows are not glass'd
We'll mind to leave the shutters fast,
the 'flight of steps requireth care'
Then why not have a hand rail there;
That feeble old and timid fair

May mount and view the prospect rare:
The blue and lofty mountain's sides
The noble bay and stealthy tides,
That treach'rous creep along the sand
Or loudly dash upon the strand

From the above verses, work out what and where this place is,
The answer to this conundrum can be found on page 94.

ACKNOWLEDGEMENTS

To John and Elizabeth, to whom I owe everything.
Thank you also to Steve, Andy and Simon who came hunting for curiosities with me, sharing many a soggy sandwich in the rainy car parks of Cumbria.

BIBLIOGRAPHY

Follies and Grottoes, Barbara Jones

Follies, a guide to rogue architecture in England, Scotland and Wales, Gywn Headley and Wim Menlenkamp.

Timpson's Towns of England and Wales

National Trust Histories: The Lake District, Chris Barringer

Secret Britain, AA

The Misericords of Carlisle Cathedral, Thirlie Grundy

Places of interest in Penrith, Beaconside CE Junior School

Gosforth Church and Cross: a Short History, the Revd David Ridgeway.

Wasdale Head, a brief history, Bill Bailey

The Good Guide to the Lakes, Hunter Davies

Answer to A CURIOSITY CONUNDRUM:–
The Hospice of Hampsfell, Cartnell
(The Greek inscription on the building means 'Rosy-fingered dawn'.)